Summary and Inference

3–4

Written by
Sarah McFadden Fornara

Editor: Joellyn Cicciarelli
Illustrator: Ann Iosa
Production: Carlie Hayashi
Cover Designer: Barbara Peterson
Art Director: Moonhee Pak
Project Manager: Collene Dobelmann
Project Director: Betsy Morris

Table of Contents

Introduction 3

DEFINING SUMMARY

Summing Up a Summary 4
Story Summaries 5
Which Story Summary Is Best? 6
Nonfiction Summaries 7
Magnets and Diamagnetic Materials 8

RESTATING MAIN IDEAS

In Other Words 9
Head in the Clouds 10
Don't Copy the Jacket 11

WRITING SUMMARIES

States of Matter 12
The Break-In 13
I'll Trade You 14
Internet Safety 15
Natural Resources 16
Moose Trail 17
What a Life! 18
Ohio's Economy 19

SUMMARY READING COMPREHENSION

Summary of Choice 20
A Whale of a Time 21
Flipping for Jenna 22
Go! Fight! Nguyen! 23
Cathay Williams 24

DEFINING MAKING INFERENCES

What I Already Know 25
Body Systems Knowledge 26
Clues from Text 27
Picture Clues 28

READING STRATEGIES FOR MAKING INFERENCES

Getting Ready 29
Picture-Perfect Question 30
Looking for Details 31
Stop and Think 32

MAKING INFERENCES PRACTICE

Emily and Spots 33
Coming to America 34
A Dog Named Winn-Dixie 35
Try, Try Again 36
Chemical and Physical Changes 37
Inferring with Experiments 38

MAKING INFERENCES READING COMPREHENSION

Helen Keller to Alexander Graham Bell 39
A New Best Friend 40
Close Encounter 41
Sir Charles the Brave 42
The Championship 43
Classifying Living Things 44
Shaun and Evan 45

Answer Key 46

Introduction

Each book in the *Power Practice*™ series contains dozens of ready-to-use activity pages to provide students with skill practice. Use the fun activities to supplement and enhance what you are teaching in the classroom. Give an activity page to students as class work, or send the pages home as homework to reinforce skills taught in class. An answer key is provided for quick reference.

The first half of this book provides students with practice in summarizing text. The ability to describe, in a few sentences, the main ideas of a nonfiction piece or fiction story is important because it helps students organize information and evaluate the importance of what they read. Students who can summarize text will be more successful when they are required to do the following: organize and remember information from text, extract important ideas from text, and create outlines and write reports. Students will make the most of study time because they can maximize the time spent on information they have not previously learned. Students use the developmentally appropriate activities and reading passages in this section to hone their summarizing skills and become better all-around readers and students.

The second half of this book helps students make inferences. When students use their prior knowledge and clues from text to fill in gaps and understand an author's unstated message, they can construct the full meaning from text. Making inferences is an important comprehension skill that helps students do the following: fully understand text, fill in omitted details from text, elaborate extensively on text, understand characters and events, compare and contrast text ideas, determine cause-and-effect relationships, identify story problems and solutions, and make logical predictions. The reproducibles in this section give students ample practice in making inferences to elevate reading comprehension.

The activities in this book are designed to be used independently. You may choose the pages that reinforce the skills or subject matter that you are currently covering. Like any good curriculum, however, you will find there is some spiraling. Topics or skill sets from earlier pages may come up again in the more advanced pages. Though it is not necessary for students to have completed the previous pages to do well, repetition of certain ideas allows you, as the teacher, to assess the success of previous instruction and to reinforce what students have already learned.

Use the ready-to-go activities to "recharge" skill review and give students the power to succeed!

Name ______________________________ Date ______________

Summing Up a Summary

A **summary** is a short statement that gives the main ideas of a selection. Only the most important parts of a selection are shared in a summary. To summarize a selection, it is essential to recognize the **main ideas**.

Read each paragraph. Circle the sentence that tells the main idea of the paragraph.

1 Gunnar woke up early. He was going to his first professional football game. The game would be at the stadium downtown. Gunnar could hardly wait!

a. The football team plays in a stadium.
b. Gunnar is going to a football game.
c. Gunnar has a brother.

2 Gunnar looked out the window. It was snowing. Would the football game be canceled? Gunnar hoped not. He would have to wear warm clothes to go to a football game in the snow. Gunnar put on heavy pants and a sweater, and went downstairs to have breakfast.

a. Gunnar looks out the window.
b. It snows during football games.
c. Gunnar prepares to watch the game in the snow.

3 At the table, Gunnar asked his dad if the game would be canceled. Gunnar's dad said, "It's still early. This storm should be over by game time. But don't worry, Gunnar. We'll see the football game, snow or no snow!"

a. Football players play in the snow.
b. Storms don't last long on days there are football games.
c. Gunnar and his dad will go to the game, snow or no snow.

4 Which sentence is the best summary of all three paragraphs? Circle your answer.

a. Gunnar got prepared to go to a football game during a snowstorm.
b. Gunnar, his brother, and his dad liked to do things together.
c. Gunnar worried a lot when the weather changed.

Name ______________________ Date ____________

Story Summaries

When you write or tell a **summary for a fiction story**, include the main ideas, such as the goals of the characters, how the characters tried to reach those goals, and whether the goals were reached. Remember, a summary is a short statement of only a few sentences.

Think about the story "Cinderella." Answer the questions to determine a good summary for the story.

1. What was each character's main goal in the story? How did he or she try to reach it?

   Cinderella ______________________

   ____

   Stepmother ______________________

   ____

   Prince ______________________

   ____

2. Which characters reached their goals?

   ______________ ______________

3. Which character did not reach his or her goal?

   ____

4. Which is the best summary for the story "Cinderella"?

   a. Cinderella was a girl who wore rags and had to clean her stepmother's house every day. Despite this, Cinderella was very beautiful and kind. This made her stepmother and stepsisters jealous and angry.

   b. Cinderella is the story of a girl who was kept as a servant of her mean stepmother. Cinderella wanted a happy life and she found it when, with the help of her fairy godmother, she went to the ball and met the prince. Cinderella left a shoe behind at the ball. The prince searched the land and finally found and married her.

Name ______________________________ Date ______________

Which Story Summary Is Best?

Remember, when you **summarize a fiction story**, include information about the characters and their goals, giving main ideas only.

Read each summary of *Charlotte's Web*. Choose the best summary. Write at least three sentences telling why you made that choice.

Summary A

Charlotte's Web is the story of farm animals that talk "animal talk." Only Fern can understand what they are saying. The story mostly takes place in the barn on Zuckerman's farm, but moves to the county fair at the end.

Summary B

Charlotte's Web is the story of a special friendship between Wilbur the pig and a spider named Charlotte. Throughout the story, Charlotte finds ways to keep Wilbur safe and alive on Zuckerman's farm. In the end, Wilbur returns the favor by caring for Charlotte's children.

I chose Summary ________. I chose this summary because ______________________

____

____

____

____

____

Name ______________________ Date ____________

Nonfiction Summaries

When you write or tell a **summary for a nonfiction article or book**, include the main ideas while leaving out unimportant details.

Read Greg's summary of an article he read that described the game of ice hockey. Draw a line through three unimportant detail sentences below to make Greg's summary better.

Hockey Summary
by Greg

British soldiers in Canada probably played the first ice hockey game in 1855. Ice hockey is a game played on an ice rink with a goal at each end. The National Hockey League (NHL) was founded in 1917. Two teams try to shoot a small rubber disk called a puck into the net of the opposite goal while trying to prevent the other team from scoring. Each year, the Stanley Cup is awarded to the best team in the NHL.

Read a nonfiction article about a sport. Write a two-sentence summary of the article including only the main ideas.

____

____

____

____

____

____

____

Name ______________________________ Date ______________

Magnets and Diamagnetic Materials

Remember, when you **summarize nonfiction**, leave out unimportant details. Only record the important main ideas.

Read this article about magnets.

Have you ever experimented with magnets? If you have, then you probably know that the opposite poles of two bar magnets (negative and positive) will be attracted to each other and stick together. If you try to put the two negative poles together, they will repel each other, or push away. The same thing happens with the positive poles.

Perhaps you have also played with magnets and other objects. Magnets are strongly attracted to objects made of metals like iron and steel. They don't stick to glass or gold. These materials may seem unaffected by magnetic fields, but they really are affected. These materials are called diamagnetic (DIE uh mag NET ik). They are actually repelled by both the negative and the positive poles of a magnet, but the force is so weak you don't notice it.

Water is another material that is diamagnetic. In fact, if you had a very powerful magnet, you could prove this by placing it near a watermelon. If the magnet were large enough, the water inside a watermelon would be repelled by the magnetic force, and you would see the watermelon roll away from the magnet.

Write **Yes** next to the best summary for this article.

_____ Some materials are diamagnetic, having a weak force that repels both the negative and positive poles of a magnet. If you have a large, powerful magnet, it is sometimes possible to move diamagnetic objects.

_____ Magnets stick to metals like iron and steel. If you have two bar magnets, the opposite poles (negative and positive) will be attracted to each other and stick together.

Write a sentence to tell why you made that choice.

____

____

____

Name ______________________________ Date ______________

In Other Words

When you write a summary, include only the main ideas **in your own words**. It is important to restate a main idea in a different way than it is presented in the text.

Read each sentence below. Rewrite the sentence in your own words. The first one is done for you.

1. You can keep your body healthy by exercising every day.

   Daily exercise keeps you healthy.

2. All of your body systems benefit from exercise.

   ____

3. Warming up before you exercise is vital to keep you from injuring muscles.

   ____

4. To avoid injury, you should not do the exact same kinds of exercise day after day.

   ____

5. When people exercise, they often get a better night's rest and feel more prepared to handle the stressful parts of their day.

   ____

   ____

Name ______________________________ Date ______________

Head in the Clouds

Remember, when you write a summary, include only the main ideas **in your own words**.

In the sky, there are high clouds, midlevel clouds, low clouds, and vertically developing clouds. Each type of cloud is classified by its appearance.

The weather is usually good when you see high cirrus clouds. These clouds are usually described as wispy and show the direction the wind is blowing. They are made of ice crystals.

Midlevel altocumulus clouds are also made of ice, but they have water in them, too. These clouds are often thick, and their dark color warns that snow or rain is likely. When people mention a blanket of clouds, they are usually referring to altocumulus clouds.

At the midlevel to lower level, there are stratocumulus clouds. These clouds are similar to the altocumulus clouds in that they are darker and usually mean rain or snow is coming. These clouds, however, consist only of water droplets—no ice.

At the lower levels, we find two different kinds of clouds: cumulus and stratus. On days when it is overcast or drizzly or there are snow flurries, you will see a layer of flat stratus clouds. Cumulus clouds are the "cotton ball" clouds you see on nice days. They usually have flat bottoms and float by quickly.

Sometimes, cumulus clouds turn into cumulonimbus clouds. When cumulonimbus clouds grow vertically, they develop into thunderheads that tower high into the sky. These clouds can bring hail, wind, or lightning with the heavy rain.

Knowing the different kinds of clouds can help you better prepare for the weather.

Restate these main ideas in your own words. You can use words from the article in new ways if you wish.

1. Cirrus clouds, made of ice crystals, are high clouds that often show the wind's direction.

____

2. Two kinds of clouds are altocumulus and stratocumulus, both of which warn of rain or snow.

____

3. Cumulus clouds, seen on nice days, and stratus clouds, seen on overcast days, are lower-level clouds.

____

Name ______________________ Date ______________

Don't Copy the Jacket

When you write main ideas for a summary, be sure to use **your own words** rather than words from the story. Never copy words from a book jacket.

Read the main idea sentences from the back of each book jacket. Rewrite the sentences in your own words.

When Justin Daniels finds out that his family is moving, he and his best friend, Amber Brown, are terribly sad and begin to fight.

____

____

____

____

Get ready to read a hilarious mystery about a dog named Harold, a very well-read cat named Chester, and a new member of the Monroe household—Bunnicula, a rabbit who just might be a vampire.

____

____

____

____

Lovable, excitable Ramona Quimby has a hard time adjusting to kindergarten and finally decides to drop out for good.

____

____

____

____

Name ______________________________ Date ______________

States of Matter

A summary always includes main ideas but *never* includes unimportant details.

Read the article. Then restate the summary in your own words. You can use words from the article in new ways if you wish.

What is matter? Matter is any substance that takes up space, has mass, and is composed of atoms and molecules. The air you breathe, the bed you sleep in, and even you are made of matter. You can't see individual atoms with the naked eye, but put together, they make everything you see. The way atoms are formed in relation to one another determines the "state" of the matter. There are three states of matter: solid, liquid, and gas.

When molecules are tightly packed together, the matter is a solid. A solid will hold its shape until force is applied against it. You may be able to break or bend it, but you can't pour it.

When you can pour matter, it is a liquid. Liquids take the shape of whatever container they're poured into. The molecules in a liquid are not as tightly packed as in a solid. Solid ice melts to become liquid water. Heat makes its molecules move farther apart.

The third state of matter is gas. In gases, the molecules and atoms are further apart from each other than those found in solids and liquids. The atoms and molecules of a gas spread out to completely fill the available space. If you continue to heat water, the molecules move faster and farther apart, which causes steam. Steam is a gas.

Summary: There are three states of matter. Matter is a solid when its molecules are close together. A liquid is a kind of matter with molecules less tightly packed than a solid. Matter is a gas when its molecules are far apart and can easily fill space.

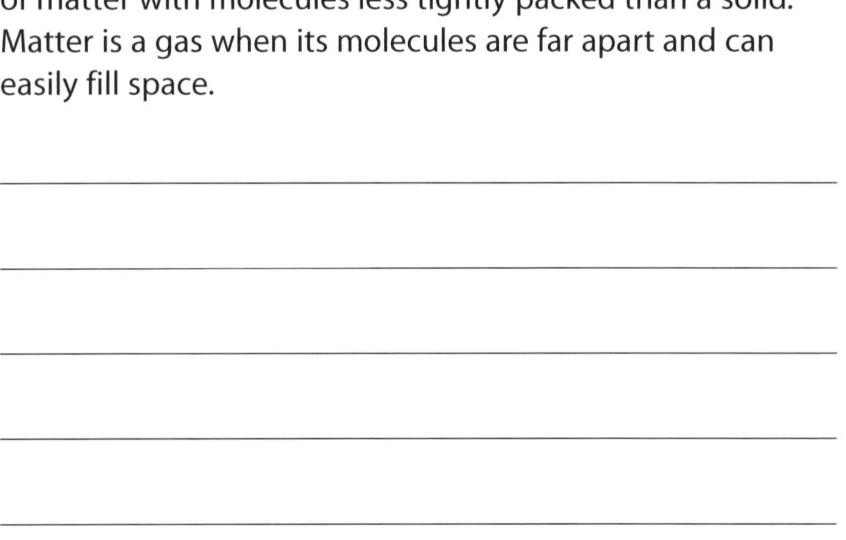

Name ____________________ Date ____________

The Break-In

A well-written **story summary** often includes the goals of the characters, how the characters tried to reach their goals, and whether the goals were reached. A summary is a short statement that gives main ideas only.

Read the story. Complete the story summary in your own words.

Last Thursday, while walking home from school, Alyssa had an idea that turned out to be a bad one. Alyssa invited Katie to her grandma's house, a place she only went on days when her mother would be home late from work. Alyssa wasn't supposed to go to Grandma's that day, but she thought it might be nice to stop by.

When Alyssa and Katie got to Grandma's, no one was home. Alyssa used her key to get in, and both girls decided to wait for Grandma. While waiting, they let the dog out (without a leash) and had a feast of cookies and chocolate milk (which they spilled). When Grandma did not come home after an hour, the girls decided to walk home.

When they reached their street, they noticed a police car with lights flashing. Running up to see what was happening, Alyssa and Katie were greeted by their mothers. "Where have you been?" Katie's mother asked tearfully. "We are so relieved to see you're okay!" Alyssa's mother added, "And did you hear? Some thieves broke into Grandma's house and stole, of all things, only milk and cookies!"

Seeing their sobbing mothers, the girls knew they had to tell the truth. They told their parents and the police what happened. From that day on, the girls always went exactly where they were supposed to go after school.

Summary:

Last Thursday, Alyssa and Katie ____________________

____________________.

In the end, ____________________

____________________.

Name ______________________ Date ____________

I'll Trade You

When you write a summary for a **nonfiction article or book**, only tell the main ideas and leave out unimportant details.

Read the article. Complete the summary in your own words.

Throughout history, people from different cultures have found ways to interact. Sometimes traders looked for others to buy their goods. Sometimes settlers encountered native peoples already inhabiting lands they wished to claim. Often, when people of different cultures meet, they learn from each other. They exchange ideas, goods, and customs, sometimes even making these new ideas part of their own cultures.

The trade route known as the Silk Road, which stretched from Europe to China, was the source of cultural exchange from about 200 A.D. to 1200 A.D. This was a trade route where people from different regions of the world could talk and share ideas. Without the cultural exchange from the Silk Road, people in Europe would not have spices like cinnamon and ginger, and people in China would not have glass. Similarly, trade across the Sahara desert, beginning around 700 A.D., linked Africa to Europe.

Around 300 A.D., the Roman Empire stretched from Iran to Spain and from Great Britain to Egypt. Roman soldiers traveled to different lands, bringing their traditions with them. As the years passed, the Roman traditions mixed with the local traditions. You can still see examples of Roman culture in these countries.

America is called the "melting pot." This is because people from many cultures come here, bringing their own customs and traditions. Over time, different aspects of these cultures become part of the overall American culture. We can learn something from almost every person we meet. The more we make friends with people from various cultures, the better we can understand their customs and traditions, making our lives much richer.

Summary:

Since early times, people from other cultures have been ______________________

____.

When we learn from other cultures, we ______________________

____.

Name ______________________________ Date ______________

Internet Safety

Read the article. Complete the summary in your own words.

The Internet can be a wonderful tool to help you learn and have fun. There are, however, some dangers that come with using the Internet. Knowing a few simple safety tips will help you stay safe.

The first rule is to make sure that you don't share personal information online. Never give your full name, address, telephone number, or name and location of your school to anyone over the Internet. If you want to enter a contest online or visit a Web site that requires information such as your e-mail, be sure to have your parents or a guardian with you. Let them help you decide if it is a safe choice.

The second thing to remember is never exchange e-mails or instant messages with people who you do not know. That way, you will not run the risk of having contact with someone who could be dangerous.

Finally, if you see anything scary or inappropriate on the Internet, tell an adult. If you see things that make you uncomfortable or confused, tell an adult. If you get a mean or angry e-mail from someone, tell an adult. If someone tells you not to share information with your parents, that is a big clue that the person is doing something wrong.

By being careful about what you see and do, you can enjoy all that the Internet has to offer. It can be a good way to learn or express your ideas. Just remember to follow certain rules to keep you safe.

Summary:

While using the Internet, ______________________________

____

______________________________.

Never ______________________________

____

______________________________.

Tell ______________________________

____

______________________________.

Name ______________________________ Date ______________

Natural Resources

Read the article. Complete the summary in your own words.

Do you eat food? Do you wear clothes? These questions may seem silly, but if we didn't have natural resources, we wouldn't have any of these things. Everything we eat and wear involves the use of natural resources.

Are you having a sandwich for lunch today? Without natural resources, you wouldn't have bread for that sandwich. Bread is made from wheat. The wheat needs minerals like phosphorus and potassium in the soil to help it grow. Wheat also needs water, another natural resource. The farmer needs gasoline from petroleum to run the combine to harvest the wheat. The combine itself is made of steel, plastic, and glass, which all come from natural resources. Many natural resources have already been used before the wheat is even close to becoming bread!

The mill that grinds the wheat into flour and the bakery where the flour is made into bread use electricity. The electricity probably comes from burning coal, another natural resource.

More natural resources are needed to make the plastic bag for your bread. The truck that drives the bread to the store needs gasoline, too. It takes a lot of natural resources just to get that bread into your lunch box.

You can conserve natural resources in many ways. An easy way to conserve is to pay attention to how much you waste natural resources. Turning off electricity when you aren't using it saves natural resources. Riding a bike or walking instead of driving a car conserves resources. Taking shorter showers and not running the water while you brush your teeth means there will be more of that resource. Another terrific way to use natural resources wisely is to recycle. When we reuse natural resources instead of wasting them, we insure that there are enough natural resources for everyone on the planet.

Summary:

We need natural resources for ______________________________

____

______________________________.

We can conserve natural resources by ______________________________

____

______________________________.

Name ______________________________ Date ______________

Moose Trail

A well-written **story summary** often includes the goals of the characters, how the characters tried to reach those goals, and whether the goals were reached. Remember, a summary is a short statement that gives main ideas only.

Read the story. Then write a summary of the story in your own words.

Jimmy and his dad, Mr. Collins, were camping in the Canadian wilderness. At the wilderness park entrance, they noticed a sign that said, *Camp in designated camping sites only*. Both Jimmy and his father chose to ignore the sign and camp in their own "perfect location."

After hours of hiking, Mr. Collins said to his son, "Jimmy, I think we've found our perfect location! Look at this nice open spot. We're near the river, and the ground is flat and dry." Jimmy agreed, and he and his father set up the tent.

A clear, calm, starry night came after a delicious dinner cooked over an open fire. Jimmy and his father decided to crawl into the tent and go to sleep. Hours passed quietly until. . . RUMBLE, RUMBLE, RUMBLE! "Is that a train?" Jimmy shouted, disoriented and frightened. "Oh no!" shouted his dad. "We're camping on a moose trail!"

Jimmy and his father rushed out of the tent and climbed high into a tree just in time to avoid being trampled by a herd of moose racing toward the river. Jimmy and Mr. Collins shivered in silence for an hour while they waited for the moose herd to have their fill of water and wander off. As they climbed down from the tree, they noticed that the mighty creatures had destroyed their tent and all their gear.

"I guess we'll let the parks choose the perfect locations from now on," said Jimmy to his dad. "You're right, son," said Mr. Collins. "Let's clean up and go home."

Summary:

____

____

____

____

____

____

Name ______________________________ Date ______________

What a Life!

Read each paragraph. Write a one- or two-sentence summary of each one.

1. The butterfly begins life hatching from an egg, which an adult butterfly laid on a leaf. The caterpillar, or larva, emerges from the egg and begins eating. It must store lots of energy for the changes ahead. When the larva is ready, it attaches itself in a safe place and forms a hard shell, known as a chrysalis, that surrounds it. This is the pupa stage. Within the chrysalis, the larva changes into a butterfly. The adult comes out of the chrysalis ready to mate and produce eggs of its own.

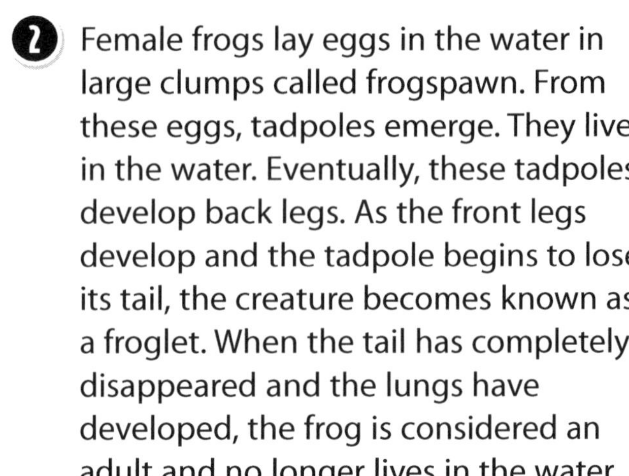

2. Female frogs lay eggs in the water in large clumps called frogspawn. From these eggs, tadpoles emerge. They live in the water. Eventually, these tadpoles develop back legs. As the front legs develop and the tadpole begins to lose its tail, the creature becomes known as a froglet. When the tail has completely disappeared and the lungs have developed, the frog is considered an adult and no longer lives in the water.

____

____

____

____

____

____

____

____

Name ______________________________ Date ______________

Ohio's Economy

When you write a summary of a **nonfiction article or book**, write the main ideas in your own words and leave out unimportant details.

Read the article. Write a summary of the article in your own words.

Economy is the use of resources such as money, goods, and materials. Ohio's economy includes both manufactured and agricultural goods. Steel is manufactured in many places near Lake Erie. The raw materials are then shipped on freighters across the water. Akron is known for producing rubber products, such as tires. Smuckers jams and jellies are made in Orville, Ohio. Cincinnati is the home of Procter and Gamble, which makes products from diapers to shampoo. Additional things manufactured in Ohio include chemicals, molded plastic, and machine tools.

Corn is an important crop in Ohio. Corn is not just used to feed animals and people. It can be turned into ethanol to run automobiles. Soybeans are another important Ohio crop. Soybeans can be eaten or made into oil for cooking. Soybeans are also used to make crayons and makeup. Animals raised in Ohio include poultry, hogs, and cattle.

If you visit Ohio, you will see an economy that allows people to earn a living in many different ways. Some people work on farms, growing corn or raising pigs. Fisherman work on Lake Erie, catching perch and walleye. Still others work in factories and make things like tires and steel.

Summary:

____

____

____

____

____

____

____

____

Name ______________________ Date ______________

Summary of Choice

When taking a reading test, you will sometimes be asked to choose the best summary and give reasons for your choice. When you read **fictional text**, it's important to choose the summary that tells about the characters' main goals.

Circle the best summary for each story.

1 Kiley and Maria decided to make breakfast in bed for their parents. Kiley said, "Let's make hard-boiled eggs in the microwave!" Maria agreed. The girls placed two eggs in a bowl, and set the oven for two minutes. Suddenly, there was an explosion! Gooey egg and bits of shell covered the inside of the microwave. The girls finished cleaning up just before their parents came downstairs. Kiley and Maria decided to help their mother prepare breakfast instead of making it themselves. They knew it was time to learn.

Summaries:

a. Kiley and Maria shouldn't have been playing around in the kitchen.

b. Kiley and Maria accidentally made exploding eggs while trying to make breakfast for their parents.

2 It was Miguel's first track meet, and the coach had placed him in the 800-meter race. Miguel had never run a half mile before and wasn't sure what to expect. As the starting gun sounded, he took off, barreling ahead of all the other runners. About halfway through the race, Miguel felt like his legs were made of lead. His body slowed to a crawl. All the runners passed Miguel, and he finished last. "Don't worry, Miguel," said his coach. "You learned a lesson today. You 'hit the wall.' Next race, pace yourself, and sprint only at the end." Miguel remembered the advice and never 'hit the wall' again.

Summaries:

a. Miguel learned a lesson about pacing himself when he ran an 800-meter race too quickly and 'hit the wall.'

b. Miguel was a new runner full of energy and excitement who could run really fast but not very far.

Name ____ Date ________________

A Whale of a Time

When being tested on your ability to summarize a reading selection, you will sometimes be asked to choose the best summary and give reasons for your choice. When you read **nonfiction text**, it's important to choose the summary that includes the main ideas but leaves out unimportant details.

Circle the best summary for each paragraph. Then complete each sentence to explain your choice.

1 Blue whales are big and loud. They are bigger than any other creature on Earth today. Their underwater communications are louder than a jet engine and carry for hundreds of miles. These vocalizations also help them find food. Blue whales are baleen whales, which feed on small fish, plankton, and krill. These whales are an endangered species even though they can be found in all of the world's oceans.

Summaries:

a. Blue whales are baleen whales, which filter out small sea creatures to eat.

b. The endangered blue whale is the biggest and loudest creature on the planet.

I chose Summary ______ because __________

____

____.

2 Right whales got their name from the early whalers who hunted them. Because these mammals were slow swimmers and had lots of the blubber the whalers wanted, they were the "right" ones to catch. Right whales are baleen whales, but unlike blue or humpback whales, they are always feeding. They are skimmers, whales who swim slowly with their mouths open to catch any plankton or krill. Since they were hunted so much, right whales are now endangered.

Summaries:

a. Right whales were the "right" ones to catch.

b. Right whales are baleen whales that have suffered from overhunting and are now endangered.

I chose Summary ______ because __________

____

____.

Name ________________________________ Date ______________

Flipping for Jenna

Read the story. Then circle the best answer for each question.

Robby was only five, but he wanted to do everything that his big sister, Jenna, could do. Jenna could play soccer, she could roller skate, and she could even do a flip off the diving board at the neighborhood pool! He wanted to show Jenna that he could act like a big kid, too, so he decided that he would teach himself to do a front flip off the diving board.

Learning to do a front flip wouldn't be easy, however, since Robby only went to the pool twice a week for lessons. That's why, every morning for a week, Robby secretly stacked pillows and blankets on the family room floor and tossed himself off the couch headfirst into the heap while his mother wasn't looking.

The next time their mother took them to the pool, Robby headed straight for the diving board. Before his mother or Jenna could stop him, he was standing at the end of the diving board. "Jenna, watch me!" he shouted. "Wait!" Jenna called. "What are you doing?"

"You'll see," said Robby. Then he flipped into the water. Jenna dove into the water to guide him to the edge of the pool. "I'm a big kid, too, Jenna!" said Robby. "You sure are!" smiled Jenna.

1. What does Robby want to do in this story?
   a. be the best diver at the pool
   b. show his sister that he is a big kid
   c. make his mother mad by jumping on the couch

2. How does Robby achieve his goal?
   a. by practicing all week in his family room
   b. by taking secret diving lessons
   c. by learning to read

3. Which sentence gives the best summary for the story?
   a. Robby is a brave boy who loves his sister.
   b. Robby practices flips every day.
   c. Robby shows that he is a big boy by doing a flip off the diving board.

Name ______________________ Date ____________

Go! Fight! Nguyen!

Read the article about Dat Nguyen. Then answer the questions.

Dat Nguyen is a football player who was drafted by the Dallas Cowboys in 1999. He played for the Cowboys until he retired in March of 2006. But All-American Nguyen's story began in far-off Vietnam. His family escaped Vietnam during the end of the Vietnam War by taking a boat to Thailand. Later, they came to the United States. Dat was born in a refugee camp in September 1975.

Nguyen's early life was filled with hard work. His family caught shrimp along the Gulf Coast near Rockport, Texas. Nguyen admits that, as a kid, he didn't always make good choices about the people he hung out with or the things that he did. He did learn, however, to work hard and to do his best on the football field.

Although considered small for a football player and not particularly fast, Nguyen's hard-hitting style earned him lots of records and awards on the field. As a college player at Texas A & M University, he averaged nearly eleven tackles per game. In 2001, he had his first full season with the Cowboys. As a middle linebacker, he racked up 172 tackles that year. Only one other player in the Cowboys' history had that many tackles in a single season.

Unfortunately, that hard-hitting style caught up with Nguyen. In 2005, knee and neck injuries forced him onto the injured reserve list. No longer able to give football his all, Nguyen chose to retire. He remains an example of how hard work and dedication can make anything possible.

1. Which sentence summarizes Dat Nguyen's early life?
   a. Dat Nguyen and his family worked hard to make a new life for themselves in the United States.
   b. Dat Nguyen played football every day after school in order to get good at it.

2. Which sentence summarizes Dat Nguyen's football career?
   a. Dat Nguyen was a hard-hitting middle linebacker who made a record number of tackles.
   b. Dat Nguyen got hurt a lot playing football and eventually had to quit the Cowboys' team.

3. Which sentence is the best summary for this article?
   a. Dat Nguyen used to be a shrimper who worked hard and did his best on the football field.
   b. Dat Nguyen is a Vietnamese American who overcame many odds to be a successful professional football player.

Name ______________________________ Date ______________

Cathay Williams

Read the story. Then answer the questions.

Around the year 1842, near Independence, Missouri, a baby girl was born to a slave woman named Martha, who was owned by William Johnson. The girl, named Cathay Williams, grew up working in the Johnson household.

During the Civil War, Union soldiers from the North took Cathay with them to do chores. She learned to cook and eventually went to work for General Sheridan. During her time with the army, she traveled and may have witnessed some important battles.

After the Civil War, Cathay needed a way to support herself, so she disguised herself as a man named William Cathay. On November 15, 1866, Cathay enlisted in the 38th Infantry, known as the Buffalo Soldiers. She went to Fort Cummings in New Mexico to protect travelers. Most likely, it was hot, boring work.

After two years, Cathay was discharged from the army. Her discharge papers say that she was discharged for poor health, and they refer to her as a man. Some believe, however, that she wished to get out of the army and allowed herself to be discovered. Since it was illegal for women to be in the army, she would have been discharged if anyone found out.

After leaving the army, Cathay once more supported herself by cooking and doing laundry. Eventually, she ended up in Colorado. While living there, she applied to receive a pension, or retirement money, from the army. Her request was denied.

It is believed that later in her life she ran a boarding house in Raton, New Mexico. There, it is said, she died at the age of 82.

There are still many things we will probably never know about Cathay Williams. It is widely believed, however, that she was the first African American woman to serve in the armed forces.

1. Which sentence summarizes Cathay Williams' early life?
   - **a.** Cathay Williams was born in 1842 near Independence, Missouri.
   - **b.** Cathay Williams served as a housemaid in the home of her master until the Civil War.

2. Which sentence summarizes Cathay Williams' time as a Buffalo Soldier?
   - **a.** Cathay Williams spent her time in the army doing hot, boring work.
   - **b.** Cathay Williams served as a soldier protecting travelers at Fort Cummings.

3. Which sentence is the best summary for this article?
   - **a.** Cathay Williams was a former slave who is believed to have been the first female African American to serve in the army.
   - **b.** Cathay Williams ran a boarding house in Raton, New Mexico, and died at the age of 82.

Name ______________________ Date ______________

What I Already Know

To **make an inference** is to use what you already know, called prior knowledge, along with clues from text and pictures to fill in gaps and understand an author's unstated message. Whenever you read, use what you already know from your own experiences to help you make inferences.

Think about what you already know about everyday things like clothing, animals, and how people look. Read the paragraph. Color the picture based on your prior knowledge.

The little girl with straw-colored hair sat on the plain wooden swing. Her dress was the color of the sky. The shoes on her feet were as dark as twin lumps of coal. Her socks were like candy canes. The dog next to her was the color of chocolate.

Name ______________________________ Date ______________

Body Systems Knowledge

When you use **prior knowledge** and clues from text and pictures to fill in gaps and understand an author's unstated message, you are making an inference. Be sure to use what you already know from your own experiences to help you make inferences.

Use your prior knowledge of body systems to match the diseases to the systems that they affect.

1. _______ circulatory system (Hint: heart and blood)
2. _______ respiratory system (Hint: lungs and breathing)
3. _______ digestive system (Hint: stomach and intestines)
4. _______ nervous system (Hint: spinal cord and nerves)
5. _______ skeletal system (Hint: bones)

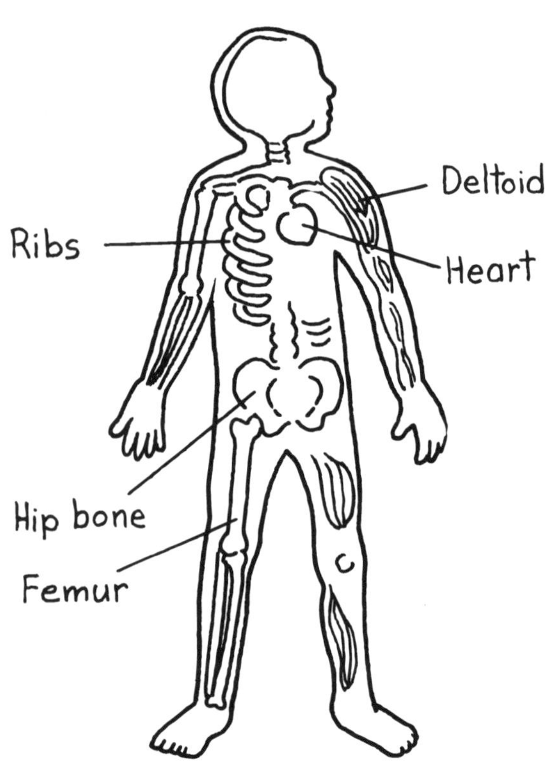

a. People with celiac disease cannot eat gluten, which is found in wheat and other grains. If they do eat things with gluten, that will damage their small intestines and keep them from absorbing other important nutrients in food.

b. Spinal muscular atrophy occurs when the nerves in the spinal cord stop sending messages to the muscles. Without these messages from the brain, the muscles weaken or may even stop working.

c. When a blood vessel that takes blood to the brain either bursts or gets clogged, a person can have a stroke. Without the blood flowing through that blood vessel, the brain can't get the oxygen and nutrients it needs.

d. Bones lose calcium and become thinner when someone has osteoporosis. Getting enough dairy products and exercising can help people avoid this disease.

e. Asthma is caused when a person's airway narrows. The person has a hard time getting the oxygen he or she needs to breathe through these smaller passageways. Many things cause asthma. Exposure to pollution or smoke can trigger asthma. It can also be the result of allergies.

Name ______________________________ Date ______________

Clues from Text

To **make an inference** is to use prior knowledge and **clues from text** and pictures to fill in gaps and understand an author's unstated message. Whenever you read, use clues from text and pictures to help you make inferences.

Read the book titles. Find a book in the left and right column that likely share the same ideas. Use the text as clues. Draw lines to match up the book pairs.

1. The Detective Finds a Clue — **a.** Fun with Chemistry
2. Lots of Laughs — **b.** Delicious Desserts
3. I Can Do Experiments — **c.** Riddles and Jokes
4. Cooking for Kids — **d.** People Long Ago
5. Take a Look at History — **e.** Solving the Mystery

Name ______________________________ Date ______________

Picture Clues

Remember, authors don't always tell you everything in the text of a book. To **make an inference** is to use prior knowledge and **clues from pictures** and text to fill in gaps and understand what the author is trying to say. Whenever you read, use clues from pictures and text to help you make inferences.

Look at the pictures. Make an inference about how each character is feeling based on the picture. Complete each sentence to tell how each character is feeling.

1.

The girl is probably feeling ______________

______________________________.

She might also be feeling ______________.

2.

The man is probably feeling ______________

______________________________.

He might also be feeling ______________.

3.

The boy is probably feeling ______________

______________________________.

He might also be feeling ______________.

4.

The woman is probably feeling ______________

______________________________.

She might also be feeling ______________.

Name ______________________ Date ____________

Getting Ready

To help you get ready to **make inferences** while reading, look through a book's pictures and read the title and cover information before starting. If a book is **nonfiction**, ask yourself, *What do I already know about this topic?* If a book is **fiction**, ask yourself, *What, if anything, do I already know about the characters and settings?*

Choose a nonfiction book and a fiction book from your classroom library. Complete the information below as you think about each book.

Nonfiction Book Title:

____

One important phrase or sentence from the cover:

____

____

The illustrations on the cover show

____

______________________.

Look through the book. Based on what you've seen so far, what do you already know about this topic?

____

____

____

Fiction Book Title:

____

One important phrase or sentence from the cover:

____

____

The illustrations on the cover show

____

______________________.

Look through the book. Based on what you've seen so far, what do you already know about this topic?

____

____

____

Name ____ Date ________________

Picture-Perfect Question

To help you **make inferences** while reading a **story supported by illustrations**, look at the picture on the page and ask yourself, *What does this picture "tell me" that isn't in the words of the story?*

Read the paragraph. Look at the picture. Then answer the question.

Sweat poured down Paul's cheeks. He wiped his brow and thought, "If I can finish this, I will have the twenty dollars I need to buy that skateboard." Paul continued to trudge along. After three hours, he was finally finished. Paul felt proud and relieved.

What does the picture "tell you" that isn't in the words in the paragraph?

____

____

____

____

____

Name ________________________________ Date ______________

Looking for Details

Remember, authors don't always tell you everything in the text of a book. To help you **make inferences** while reading a **fiction story**, look for details that help you understand the plot, the characters, and the setting of the story. Ask yourself, *What do these details tell me? What doesn't the author tell me with these details?*

Read the paragraph. Then answer the questions.

Standing there in her makeup and sparkling tutu, Keisha looked like the picture of grace and confidence. The bright lights above her glared like lightning bolts ready to strike. Keisha tried not to think about the 500 faces that stared blankly at her and her friends. Finally, the music started. Would Keisha's legs move?

1. What do the details about Keisha and the stage tell you about the activity Keisha is going to do?

____

____

2. What are some clues that tell you this?

____

____

3. What might you be able to infer about Keisha from what the details tell and don't tell?

____

____

4. What are some clues that tell you this?

____

____

Name ______________________________ Date ______________

Stop and Think

To help you **make inferences** while reading a **fiction story**, think about what you read, see, and already know to add up all the clues and fill in the gaps. This way, you can understand what the author really means. As you read, stop from time to time and ask yourself, *What did I figure out about the story that I didn't know before?*

Choose a fiction story or book that you are reading in your free time. Then follow the directions below.

Title of Story or Book: ______________________________

Page Number(s) I Read: ______________________________

1. Read for five minutes. Stop. What did you figure out about the story that you didn't know before?

____

____

____

2. Read for five more minutes. Stop. What do the details in this section tell you?

____

____

____

3. What might you be able to infer about the characters, setting, or plot from what the details tell and don't tell?

____

____

____

Name ______________________________ Date ______________

Emily and Spots

Remember, an author doesn't always tell you everything. When you read, you must "fill in" information by drawing on your prior knowledge and using clues in the text and pictures.

Read each paragraph from a story. Complete the sentences to tell the inferences you made.

1. Emily sat on the top rail of the fence. She looked out across the meadow. The hot wind blew her hair, but she didn't notice. She was too excited! Aunt Laura had said that as soon as Emily's vacation started she could come visit the farm. Now that she was here, Emily knew that all kinds of wonderful things would happen to her.

Emily is ______________________________.

The season is ______________________________.

Emily is not at home. She is ______________________________.

Emily feels ______________________________.

2. Emily heard Aunt Laura coming. The pounding of hooves carried on the breeze. Emily hoped Aunt Laura would be riding Spots. He was Emily's favorite. As Aunt Laura rode out of the woods, Emily saw that she was on Spots' back. Aunt Laura smiled and waved.

Aunt Laura is riding a ______________________________.

The animal is moving ______________________________.

Aunt Laura feels ______________________________.

3. Which horse do you think is Spots?

a.

b.

Name ______________________ Date ____________

Coming to America

When you read, make inferences by drawing on your prior knowledge and using clues in the text and pictures to discover ideas that the author does not state in the text.

Read the story and the statements that follow. Write *True* or *False* to show the inferences you made from reading.

Mia was very nervous. It was her first day in her new school. Her parents and their friend, Mrs. Brown, had brought her. Mrs. Brown spoke to the people in the office and then explained to Mia that her teacher would be Mr. Perez.

Mrs. Brown walked down the hall with Mia past a bulletin board covered with pictures of turkeys and Pilgrims. When they reached the classroom, Mr. Perez said hello to Mia and showed her to a desk. He handed her a book just like the one the other boys and girls had in their hands.

Mia looked at the front of the book. There was a picture of a boy and a dog. She opened the book. There were not very many pictures inside. Mia could not read any of the words.

Mr. Perez started to ask the other students questions about the book. Mia could not understand anything he was saying. She began to wonder if she would ever feel comfortable in this strange place.

1. ________ This story takes place in the United States.
2. ________ Mia has lots of friends at this school.
3. ________ Mrs. Brown helps people.
4. ________ It is the beginning of the school year.
5. ________ The class was in the middle of a math lesson when Mia arrived.
6. ________ The class is reading a story about a girl and her horse.
7. ________ Mia is in kindergarten.
8. ________ Mia speaks English well.
9. ________ Mia is from another country.
10. ________ Mia is uncomfortable.

Name ______________________________ Date ______________

A Dog Named Winn-Dixie

Remember to "fill in the gaps" by drawing on your prior knowledge and using clues in the text and pictures to discover ideas that the author does not state in the text.

Read the following passage from *Because of Winn-Dixie* by Kate DiCamillo. Note: Winn-Dixie is a dog, and the narrator is a girl named Opal. Opal's father is a preacher.

"Winn-Dixie looked at the preacher. He didn't smile at him, but he opened his mouth wide like he was laughing, like the preacher had just told him the funniest joke in the world; and this is what amazed me the most: The preacher laughed back. Winn-Dixie hopped on the bed, and the preacher got up and turned out the light. I leaned over and kissed Winn-Dixie, too, right on the nose, but he didn't notice. He was already asleep and snoring."

Read each sentence. Circle four sentences that you can infer from the passage above.

1. Winn-Dixie opens his mouth like he is laughing.
2. Opal's father, the preacher, doesn't laugh often.
3. Opal loves Winn-Dixie.
4. The preacher laughs back at the dog.
5. Winn-Dixie hops on the bed and goes to sleep.
6. Winn-Dixie is bringing happiness to Opal's family.
7. Winn-Dixie likes living with Opal's family.

Name ______________________________ Date ______________

Try, Try Again

Wesley did not use his prior knowledge or clues from text to make inferences about the following stories. Read each story and the inference Wesley made about it. Change each inference so it is more accurate. Write your new inference on the line, and explain what clues helped you.

1. It was almost closing time. Rusty had been in the pound for two weeks. A few people had looked at him, but they had all taken other dogs home with them. Rusty was wondering if he would ever have a family of his own when a small boy came running over to his cage.

   Wesley's inference: Rusty wants to stay in the pound.

   ____

   ____

2. Sierra moved quietly between the branches of the old pine tree. The branches were so low that they touched the ground. Inside the branches was their secret fort. Kaitlyn was already there, waiting for her. She could hardly wait to eat lunch. Sierra set down the basket and started unpacking it. First, she spread out the blanket. Then, she laid out the plates and silverware.

   Wesley's inference: Sierra and Kaitlyn met at the fort during the night.

   ____

   ____

3. Sara anxiously looked at the other girls. A few were taller than she, but she wasn't worried. Sara had been practicing with her older brother. She bounced the basketball a few times by her side and signaled to her teammates. When the whistle blew, she was ready.

   Wesley's Inference: Sara isn't excited about the basketball game.

   ____

   ____

Name ______________________________ Date ______________

Chemical and Physical Changes

Read the article. Use what you learn about chemical reactions to infer if physical or chemical changes occur in the situations below.

Everything is made up of matter, and matter is made up of molecules and atoms. How close these molecules are to one another determines the state of matter. It can be a solid, liquid, or gas. Ice melting into water and then being heated to steam is an example of a physical change. Only the distance between the molecules changes.

If molecules actually change you get something very different. When molecules change and a new substance or substances are made, you have a chemical reaction. You might think that chemical reactions involve explosions. Some do. Chemical reactions do release energy, but most chemical reactions are ordinary, everyday events. Every time you eat something, a chemical reaction is occurring. The acids in your stomach break down the molecules in the foods you eat. This gives you the energy your body needs. If your bike is left out in the rain and rusts, that is a chemical reaction. The molecules in the bike's metal are changing. All around you there are chemical reactions happening.

Write *Physical* if the change described is a physical change. Write *Chemical* if it is a chemical change.

1. ____________ You crush an aluminum can.
2. ____________ Water you spilled on the hot sidewalk evaporates.
3. ____________ You mix water and dry concrete to make cement.
4. ____________ You drop lemon juice into baking soda, and carbon dioxide bubbles start to form.
5. ____________ You melt butter in a pan.
6. ____________ You make a campfire, and smoke rises.
7. ____________ You crumple up a piece of paper.

Name ______________________________ Date ______________

Inferring with Experiments

Read the results of each experiment below. Choose the inferences that make sense according to the data collected.

1. Christopher rubbed two identical socks with a tablespoon of dirt. He washed Sock A in one-half cup of Detergent A and five gallons of water. He washed Sock B in one-half cup of Detergent B and five gallons of water. He asked 40 people which sock looked whiter after it had been washed. Thirty-seven people said Sock B looked whiter. Three people said Sock A looked whiter. What can Christopher infer?

   a. Detergent A works better than Detergent B.
   b. Detergent B works better than Detergent A.
   c. The two detergents work the same.
   d. He needs to do more experimenting.

2. Daniel bought a mouse at the pet store. He taught it to run a maze by putting cheese at the end of the maze. It took the mouse twelve tries to get through the maze to the cheese. Then, Daniel put a piece of baloney at the end of the maze. The mouse got to the baloney on the first try. What can Daniel infer?

   a. The mouse likes baloney better.
   b. The mouse likes cheese better.
   c. The mouse had already learned the maze by the time the baloney was put in.
   d. He needs to do more experimenting.

3. Kanisha filled a wide-mouthed jar three-quarters full with uncooked rice. She pushed a rubber ball from a set of jacks down into the jar until it was covered with the rice. She shook the jar back and forth ten times. When she looked in the jar, the ball was on top of the rice. She repeated the experiment four more times. Each time, the rubber ball was on top of rice. What can Kanisha infer?

   a. Rubber balls float on rice.
   b. When you have particles of two different sizes, the larger particles sink.
   c. When you have particles of two different sizes, the larger particles rise.
   d. She needs to do more experimenting.

Name ______________________________ Date ______________

Helen Keller to Alexander Graham Bell

Some reading tests will test your ability to make inferences. So, whenever you read, it's important to use what you already know (prior knowledge) and clues from text and pictures to fill in gaps and understand the author's unstated message.

Read from the real letter written to Alexander Graham Bell from Helen Keller on February 19, 1907 (*The Alexander Graham Bell Family Papers* at the Library of Congress, 1861–1939). Then answer the questions by making inferences. Explain your answers using words from the letter.

"... I am at a loss how to thank you for coming to help me in New York. So inadequate are words to express the heart's warmest emotions!

... One thing you will surely let me say. You have been and are very good to me, and so is Mrs. Bell, and though I be silent, I cherish ever the many tokens of your love.

I did not realize how difficult it would be for you to come and help me out at the meeting, especially when you had no time to read the speech over or rehearse with me. But everyone said we did splendidly, and made a beautiful picture together, and certainly a happier girl than myself was not to be found that night.

... Our New York visit was one of more than usual intensity. We had a very pleasant time. We enjoyed the whirl and gaiety of that great city. Nevertheless, it was good to return to the sunshine and the peace of our home.

We half expected to go to Washington from New York, but were too weary at the end of our visit to think of another trip. I long to be with you again and to see and hear what you are doing, and whether we are any nearer to flying...."

1. How does Helen Keller feel about Alexander Graham Bell?

   ____

2. Did it matter that they did not have time to practice together?

   ____

3. Does Helen Keller live in a busy place?

   ____

4. Where does Alexander Graham Bell live?

   ____

Name ______________________________ Date ______________

A New Best Friend

To make inferences when reading, use what you already know (prior knowledge) and clues from text and pictures to fill in gaps and understand the author's unstated message.

Read the story. Circle the best answer for each question.

It was noisy and smelly as Dylan entered the gray concrete building. The woman in uniform behind the desk looked up at him and smiled.

Dylan tried to decide if he should go into the room on the right or the room on the left first. He decided to go right and pushed open the door.

This room was a little quieter. Each metal cage held a furry body, but most of them were sleeping or just quietly looking at him. One cage's occupant was playing around with a stuffed mouse. Occasionally, a soft mewing came from a small orange and white ball of fluff in the cage closest to the door. Dylan took his time and peered carefully into each cage.

When he was done in that room, Dylan returned to the main office. He paused to look at the pictures marked "Lost," "Found," and "Free to a Good Home," hanging on the bulletin board. Then he went into the room to the left.

Yips and whines greeted Dylan's ears. Big and small; black, white, brown, and gray—there were so many choices! Some of the animals looked quiet and sad. Others leaped up and down or wagged their tails energetically. Again, Dylan took his time and looked at each one.

In the very last cage sat a bright-eyed mixed breed. He had brown ears and a white body with black spots. He looked up at Dylan expectantly, but he did not bark.

"Hello," said Dylan. He was rewarded with a tail wag.

This is the one, thought Dylan. He would go right home and ask his mom to come back with him to help fill out the adoption paperwork. In just a few hours, he and his new best friend could be playing fetch.

1. Dylan is at the ______________.
   pet store — animal shelter — zoo

2. First, Dylan went and looked at the ______________.
   cats — dogs — rabbits

3. Second, Dylan went and looked at the ______________.
   cats — dogs — rabbits

4. Dylan ______________.
   found a pet he liked — did not find a pet he liked — wasn't looking for a pet

Name ______________________________ Date ______________

Close Encounter

Remember, authors don't always tell you everything. To make inferences, look for details that help you understand the plot, the characters, and the setting of the story. Ask yourself, *What do these details tell me? What doesn't the author tell me with these details?*

Read the story. Make inferences to answer the questions.

Madelyn stood on the rocking deck of the boat. The air was cool here off the coast of northern California. The water would be colder. Madelyn zipped on her wet suit. She checked her fins and mask. Then she strapped on a full air tank and adjusted the regulator.

Once in the water, Madelyn began to explore the rocky reef. There were so many beautiful and interesting creatures to see! Madelyn was here to visit some old friends.

Soon Madelyn was swimming amongst graceful, gliding shelled giants. Pink-spotted heads jutted from the bony shells, looking intently ahead. Huge clawless flippers paddled through the waters, pushing her friends onward.

Madelyn knew that her friends were special. They were endangered due to being caught in commercial fishing nets. As Madelyn watched, she hoped that her friends would safely make their migration this summer and later in the early fall.

Madelyn wished she could introduce her gigantic friends to their cousin "Snappy." Snappy was a tiny land version of the same reptile that she kept as a pet.

As Madelyn waved good-bye, she vowed to help her friends. She would make sure that generations could continue their migrations each year, finding their way home and back in safety.

1. In what ocean is Madelyn swimming? ______________

2. What sport is Madelyn doing? ______________________

3. With what kinds of reptiles is Madelyn swimming?

____

4. What makes you think so?

____

____

Name ______________________________ Date ______________

Sir Charles the Brave

Read the story. Make inferences to answer the questions.

The trees were close together. Not much sunlight came through the leaves overhead, so it was dark and creepy even in the middle of the day. The saddle beneath Sir Charles creaked, and his armor softly clinked. Other than that, there were no sounds.

After a while, Sir Charles arrived at a clearing. The grass there was blackened. The ground was littered with animal bones. The air smelled like smoke.

Sir Charles slid from the saddle and moved forward on foot. His sword was in the scabbard at his side. He kept one hand on it as he crept toward the cave on the other side of the clearing.

As Sir Charles approached the cave, he could see someone inside. It was the princess.

"Quickly," she said to Sir Charles. "He will be back any minute now."

The princess went to a nearby jeweled chest and opened it. She started taking out golden plates and goblets.

Suddenly, they heard heavy footsteps approaching. They heard snorting and smelled a smell like an old campfire. The princess peeked from the cave.

"Get ready," she said. "Here he comes."

An enormous, dark shape filled the mouth of the cave.

"Surprise!" All of the villagers jumped out of their hiding places.

"Thank you! Thank you!" said the creature. "I thought you had forgotten my special day."

"How could we?" asked the princess. "We love you."

1. Where is Sir Charles? ______________________

2. What is Sir Charles's job? ______________________

3. What kind of creature might the story refer to? ______________________

4. How was Sir Charles traveling? ______________________

5. What is the special day? ______________________

6. Does the creature harm the villagers? ______________________

Name ______________________ Date ______________

The Championship

Read the story. Make inferences to answer the questions.

It was the Tigers' first shot at the championship, and they wanted to win it all. They defeated the Sharks and the Panthers. They squeaked by the Mustangs. At last, they made it to the finals.

The Tigers knew the Racers would be a tough team to beat. They were like a well-oiled machine. They knew how to get the ball down the field. Once it was near the goal, someone almost always passed it to Pedro, who easily scored.

Mr. Watson gathered the team around him before the game. "Work together as a team," he said. "Always know where the ball is, and be ready."

It was a difficult game. The Tigers had a tough time keeping up with the Racers as they sped up and down the field. They worked as a team and were able to pass and move the ball.

At halftime, the score was one to one. When the whistle blew for the second half, they were ready to go again. The second half did not go so well for them. The Racers had worn out the Tigers. Bobby, the Tigers' best player, tried again and again to get the ball past the Racers. Meanwhile, the Racers scored three more times. When the whistle blew to end the game, the Tigers' hearts sank. Howie threw the ball into the next field as hard as he could.

"Hey," said Mr. Watson. "Don't worry. We will practice hard and get them next year."

1. For how many years have the Tigers been champions?

   ____

2. Which team almost beat the Tigers in the semifinals?

   ____

3. Who is the Racers' best player?

   ____

4. Do other teams often get within scoring distance of the Racers' goal?

   ____

5. Who is Mr. Watson?

   ____

6. Which team has faster runners?

   ____

Name ______________________________ Date ______________

Classifying Living Things

Read the article. Make inferences to answer the questions.

Do you have a collection at home? How do you organize it? Take a walk around your neighborhood and you will see many plants and animals. How do scientists organize all the living things in the world?

Scientists can classify plants based on how they reproduce, or make new plants. Some plants, like ferns, make spores. Other plants make seeds. You have probably planted seeds and watched them grow into new plants. Another way scientists classify plants is based on whether they are vascular or nonvascular. A vascular plant is one with parts that look like tubes. You have probably seen these tubes in celery. The tubes move water from the roots to the leaves.

Scientists classify animals according to whether or not they have a backbone or spine. Another name for animals with backbones is vertebrates. Birds, mammals, reptiles, fish, and amphibians are all vertebrates. Animals without backbones, or invertebrates, include animals like worms; spiders; insects; mollusks, like clams and squid; and crustaceans, like crabs.

Scientists can also classify animals according to what they eat. Carnivores eat meat, herbivores eat plants, and omnivores eat both. Finally, animals can be either warm-blooded or cold-blooded. Warm-blooded animals are able to keep their bodies the same temperature. Cold-blooded animals have body temperatures that change according to how warm or cold their environments are.

1. How do nonvascular plants, like green algae and moss, get water?
   a. They don't need water.
   b. They take in water through all their parts.
   c. They have tubes in their stems.

2. What would an insectivore eat?

   ____

3. Humans have a body temperature of about 98.6°F most of the time, unless they are sick. Are humans warm-blooded or cold-blooded?

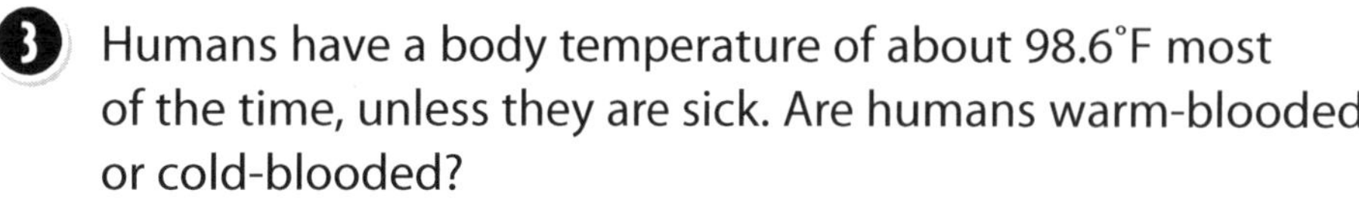

   ____

Name ______________________________ Date ______________

Shaun and Evan

Read the story. Make inferences to answer the questions.

Shaun was excited! His best friend, Evan, was coming over after school. They were going to have so much fun!

The doorbell rang. "I'll get it, Mom," Shaun shouted as he raced toward the door.

When he opened the door, Evan and his mom were at the top of the ramp.

"Hi, Shaun," said Evan's mom. "Thanks for having Evan over. We came straight from school, so Evan will need a snack first before he can play."

Evan and his mom came in the house. While Shaun ate some graham crackers and milk, Evan's mom hooked up Evan's feeding tube. When both boys had full tummies, they went off to play.

Evan moved his power chair down the hall to Shaun's room. Shaun had the action figures already set up on a table. He handed one to Evan. They played with the action figures for a while and then decided to go outside.

Evan went down the ramp and onto the driveway. Shaun got the soccer ball. The boys played soccer. Shaun kicked the ball to Evan, and then Evan dribbled the ball down to the goal.

When they were tired, the boys went back inside. Shaun put the joystick on Evan's tray, and they played video games.

"Time to go, Evan," his mom smiled.

"Do I have to?" asked Evan.

"I'm afraid so. But you can have Shaun come over tomorrow."

Shaun walked out to the van with Evan, and they talked while Evan's mom put down the lift. "I'll see you tomorrow," said Shaun.

"I can't wait," said Evan. "We will have even more fun than today."

1. Why did Shaun's house have a ramp at the front door?

____

____

2. What does Evan have difficulty doing?

   playing video games   chewing food   reading

3. Why would Shaun have the action figures set up on a table rather than on the floor?

____

____

Answer Key

Summing Up a Summary (page 4)

1. b
2. c
3. c
4. a

Story Summaries (page 5)

1. Answers will vary. Possible answers include: Cinderella's main goal was to live a happy life. She went to the ball with the help of a fairy godmother.

The stepmother's main goal was to stop Cinderella from going to the ball. She made her stay home and clean.

The prince's main goal was to marry Cinderella. He searched the land with her shoe.

2. Cinderella and the prince
3. the stepmother
4. b

Which Story Summary Is Best? (page 6)

Possible answer:
I chose Summary B. I chose this summary because it best summed up the main idea of the story and included information about the main characters and their goals.

Nonfiction Summaries (page 7)

Lines should be drawn through the following sentences:
British soldiers in Canada probably played the first ice hockey game in 1855.

The National Hockey League was founded in 1917.

Each year the Stanley Cup is awarded to the best team in the NHL.

Summaries will vary.

Magnetic and Diamagnetic Materials (page 8)

Students should write *Yes* next to the following: Some materials are diamagnetic, having a weak force that repels both the negative and positive poles of a magnet. If you have a large, powerful magnet, it is sometimes possible to move diamagnetic objects.

Sentences will vary.

In Other Words (page 9)

Answers will vary. Possible answers include:
2. Exercise keeps your body systems in good health.
3. Avoid muscle injuries by warming up before you exercise.
4. Vary your daily workouts to avoid injury.
5. Exercise helps regulate your sleep patterns and enables you to handle stress better.

Head in the Clouds (page 10)

Answers will vary. Possible answers include:
1. High clouds include cirrus clouds that are made of ice crystals and often show the direction of the wind.
2. Altocumulus and stratocumulus clouds are clouds that warn us of rain or snow.
3. Lower-level clouds include cumulus clouds, which you see on nice days, and stratus clouds, which you see on overcast days.

Don't Copy the Jacket (page 11)

Answers will vary. Possible answers include:
Justin Daniel's family is going to move. He and Amber Brown, his closest friend, are very sad. They even start to fight.

If you like a little comedy with your mystery story, read about Harold the dog, Chester the literate cat, and Bunnicula. This bunny might be a vampire!

Ramona Quimby, a likable and energetic kindergartener, decides she is not going back to school ever again!

States of Matter (page 12)

Answers will vary. Possible answer:
The three states of matter are solid, liquid, and gas. Solids have tightly packed molecules. Liquids have molecules that are farther apart. Liquids cannot hold a shape. Gases have molecules that are the farthest apart. Gases can easily fill space.

The Break-In (page 13)

Possible answer:
Last Thursday, Alyssa and Katie went to Alyssa's grandma's when no one was home. In the end, the girls learned an important lesson—always go exactly where you are expected to go.

I'll Trade You (page 14)

Possible answer:
Since early times, people from other cultures have been exchanging ideas, goods, and customs. When we learn from other cultures, we make our lives better and more interesting.

Internet Safety (page 15)

Possible answer:
While using the Internet, keep your personal information to yourself. Never exchange e-mails or instant messages with strangers. Tell a grown-up if something unusual or scary happens while you're on the Internet.

Natural Resources (page 16)

Possible answer:
We need natural resources for nearly everything we do and have. We can conserve natural resources by riding our bikes, limiting the water we use, and turning off electricity we aren't using.

Moose Trail (page 17)

Possible answer:
Jimmy and his dad didn't follow the rules and camped in the wrong spot. They were nearly trampled by a herd of moose.

What a Life! (page 18)

Answers will vary. Possible answers include:

1. A butterfly has four stages in its life: egg, larva, pupa, and adult.
2. Frogs begin as eggs. They then turn into tadpoles and later froglets. Froglets finally become adults.

Ohio's Economy (page 19)

Possible answer:
People in Ohio earn money in many ways, including making things like steel and rubber, farming, and raising animals.

Summary of Choice (page 20)

1. b
2. a

A Whale of a Time (page 21)

1. b

Possible answer: I chose Summary b because it describes blue whales without using extra details.

2. b

Possible answer: I chose Summary b because it explains the main ideas of the paragraph without giving unimportant details.

Flipping for Jenna (page 22)

1. b
2. a
3. c

Go! Fight! Nguyen! (page 23)

1. a
2. a
3. b

Cathay Williams (page 24)

1. b
2. b
3. a

What I Already Know (page 25)

Picture should be colored as follows: hair, yellow; swing, brown; dress, blue; shoes, black; socks, red and white; dog, brown.

Body Systems Knowledge (page 26)

1. c
2. e
3. a
4. b
5. d

Clues from Text (page 27)

1. e
2. c
3. a
4. b
5. d

Picture Clues (page 28)

Answers will vary. Possible answers include:

1. The girl is probably feeling sad. She might also be feeling angry.
2. The man is probably feeling nervous. He might also be feeling excited.
3. The boy is probably feeling happy. He might also be feeling proud.
4. The woman is probably feeling surprised. She might also be feeling angry.

Getting Ready (page 29)

Answers will vary.

Picture-Perfect Question (page 30)

Possible answer:
The picture tells me that Paul is mowing a huge lawn, and that is why he is hot, tired, and sweaty.

Looking for Details (page 31)

Answers will vary. Possible answers include:

1. They tell me that she is going to be in a dance recital.
2. She is wearing a tutu. 500 faces stared at her.
3. She is nervous.
4. She tried not to think about the 500 faces. Would Keisha's legs move?

Stop and Think (page 32)

Answers will vary.

Emily and Spots (page 33)

1. Emily is outside. The season is summer. Emily is not at home. She is visiting her Aunt Laura. Emily feels happy.
2. Aunt Laura is riding a horse. The animal is moving quickly. Aunt Laura feels glad to see Emily.
3. a

Coming to America (page 34)

1. True
2. False
3. True
4. False
5. False
6. False
7. False
8. False
9. True
10. True

A Dog Named Winn-Dixie (page 35)

Students should circle sentences 2, 3, 6, and 7.

Try, Try Again (page 36)

Answers will vary. Possible answers include:

1. Rusty wants to find a home. The clue can be "Rusty was wondering if he would ever have a family of his own."
2. Sierra and Kaitlyn met around noon. The clue can be "She could hardly wait to eat lunch."
3. Sara is excited to play the basketball game. The clue can be "When the whistle blew, she was ready."

Chemical and Physical Changes (page 37)

1. Physical
2. Physical
3. Chemical
4. Chemical
5. Physical
6. Chemical
7. Physical

Inferring with Experiments (page 38)

1. b
2. c
3. c

Helen Keller to Alexander Graham Bell (page 39)

Answers will vary. Possible answers include:

1. Helen likes him. She says he is very good to her.
2. No. Everyone says they did splendidly.
3. No. It is peaceful.
4. Washington. They were going to go there.

A New Best Friend (page 40)

1. animal shelter
2. cats
3. dogs
4. found a pet he liked

Close Encounter (page 41)

1. Pacific
2. scuba diving
3. Sea turtles (Pacific leatherbacks)
4. Possible answer: The way she described the shells and flippers makes me think they are turtles.

Sir Charles the Brave (page 42)

Answers will vary. Possible answers include:

1. in a forest
2. knight
3. a fire-breathing dragon
4. on horseback
5. It's the dragon's birthday.
6. no

The Championship (page 43)

1. None. It was their first shot.
2. the Mustangs
3. Pedro
4. no
5. the Tigers' coach
6. the Racers

Classifying Living Things (page 44)

1. b
2. insects
3. warm-blooded

Shaun and Evan (page 45)

1. Evan could use it; he's in a wheelchair
2. chewing food
3. Evan is in a wheelchair and can't get on the floor easily.